# Back-to-School Safety

### by Lisa M. Herrington

### Content Consultant
Debra Holtzman, J.D., M.A.

### Reading Consultant
Jeanne Clidas, Ph.D.
Reading Specialist

**Children's Press®**
An Imprint of Scholastic Inc.
New York Toronto London Auckland Sydney
Mexico City New Delhi Hong Kong
Danbury, Connecticut

Dear Parent/Educator:
It is very important that children learn how to be safe when heading back to school. However, this is something they might need help with from a grown-up. If your child needs that help, we hope you will use this book as a springboard to a discussion about back-to-school safety with him or her. You can read the book together the first time, and talk about the different suggestions inside.

Library of Congress Cataloging-in-Publication Data
Herrington, Lisa M.
Back-to-school safety / by Lisa M. Herrington.
  p. cm. — (Rookie read-about safety)
 Includes index.
 ISBN 978-0-531-28967-9 (library binding) — ISBN 978-0-531-29269-3 (pbk.)
 1. Schools—Safety measures—Juvenile literature. I. Title.
 LB2864.5.H47 2012
 363.11'9371—dc23                                               2012013372

Produced by Spooky Cheetah Press

1 2 3 4 5 6 7 8 9 10 R 22 21 20 19 18 17 16 15 14 13

Photographs © 2013: iStockphoto: 27 (Christopher Futcher), cover (Svetlana Braun), 3 top, 31 top left (Vassiliy Mikhailin); PhotoEdit/David Young-Wolff: 19; Thinkstock: 14 (Adam Crowley), 4 (Digital Vision), 3 bottom, 20, 31 bottom left, 31 bottom right (iStockphoto), 7, 11, 24, 28 (Jupiterimages), 23 (Jupiterimages/Getty Images), 31 top right (Steve Mason), 8, 12, 17.

# Table of Contents

TODAY'S LESSON: MATH

3+3=
3+2=
3+1

2+5=
3+5=

4

# Ready for School!

Ready to head back to school? Find out how to have a fun and safe year.

Do not overload your backpack.
Pack only what you need.
Always wear both straps.

# Ride Safe

If you take the bus, stay out of the street. Stand back from the curb while you wait.

Stay seated on the bus. Do not jump, run, or make loud noises. That might distract the driver.

Keep the bus aisle clear.
Backpacks block the way.
Kids can trip on them.

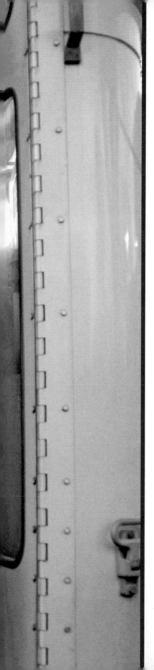

Wait for the bus to make a complete stop. Then get off. Hold on to the handrail as you exit the bus.

You might have to cross in front of the bus. Be sure the driver can see you, and you can see the driver. **If you drop something in the street, do not ever stop to pick it up.** Never walk behind the bus.

# Walk This Way

Do you walk to school?
Always obey the crossing guard.

Use crosswalks to cross the street.
Look **left, right, left** before you
cross. Never run out into the street
or between parked cars.

# In-School Rules

You need to be safe at school, too.
Do not run in the hall. You can fall.

Treat others with kindness and respect. Tell an adult if someone is mean to you or another child.

Be careful on the playground. Follow the playground rules. Play nicely with others.

Listen for instructions in case of a fire drill or an emergency. Follow these rules for a safe and great year!

**Try It!** Read the tips on page 21 again. Practice looking left, right, left, as if you are crossing the street.

# I Can Be Safe!

- Do not carry too much in your backpack.

- Never walk behind the school bus.

- Look left, right, left when crossing streets.

- Follow the rules on the playground.

# Words You Know

backpack

crossing guard

playground

school bus

31

# Index

# Facts for Now

Visit this Scholastic Web site for more information on back-to-school safety:
**www.factsfornow.scholastic.com**
Enter the keyword **School**

# About the Author

Lisa M. Herrington writes print and digital materials for kids, teachers, and parents. She lives in Connecticut with her husband and daughter. She hopes all kids stay safe!